FANTASTIC BEASTS AND WHERE TO FIND THEM

NIFFLER

A BEHIND-THE-SCENES GUIDE TO THE CREATURE AND FELLOW CHARACTERS ON FILM

BY RAMIN ZAHED

A Division of Insight Editions, LP
San Rafael, California

MEET THE NIFFLER

The Niffler is one of the many charming and unusual creatures featured in *Fantastic Beasts and Where to Find Them*. The film depicts it as a rodent-like beast with a long snout and covered in a coat of dark fur. Nifflers love to dig for gold and other shiny objects and can cause a lot of damage in human households and environments. In the film, the Niffler plays a key role and is the catalyst for Newt Scamander's adventures in New York. Eddie Redmayne, who plays Newt in the film, explains, "They have this wonderful love-hate relationship. The Niffler is incredibly aggravating and wonderful at the same time."

THE BANK INCIDENT

When the Niffler escapes from Newt's case and wreaks havoc in the Steen National Bank, Newt chases the creature into the bank's safe, which is full of shiny objects. The chase eventually ends with the unfortunate switch of Newt's and Jacob's cases in the alleyway outside the bank. To help the actors interact with the Niffler realistically, the production team built a puppet as a stand-in. Then, the Visual Effects team, led by supervisors Tim Burke and Christian Manz, removed the puppet and replaced it with an animated digital version of the character.

NEWT SCAMANDER

Newt Scamander is the main hero of *Fantastic Beasts and Where to Find Them*. The film is set seventy years before the events that occur in *Harry Potter and the Sorcerer's Stone*. Newt is a Magizoologist, a person who studies magical beasts.

The film centers on Newt as a young man as he travels to New York City in 1926. Actor Eddie Redmayne says he was captivated by this magical new adventure penned by J.K. Rowling: "This world, it's been a wonder really—it's just unlike anything I've ever been a part of."

Eddie says he also has grown very fond of Newt's character. "I like his sense of wonder and the way he takes things as he sees them. I'm not sure that he's particularly good with human beings, but he's at peace, and he's most comfortable in his skin when he's with animals—when he is down in his case."

A Loyal Friend

Although few details are known about Newt's life before the time of the movie, there is no doubt about his love for the fantastic beasts he studies. He is a kind-hearted, courageous man who wears his outsider badge with honor. As Eddie explains, "He's an excellent Magizoologist, and ultimately, a loyal friend. Obviously, Newt cares passionately about magical creatures. He'll go anywhere in the world to find them. And he'll do anything to protect them. In a way, he knows his beasts better than he knows himself. He certainly understands beasts better than he does people!"

CREATURE FEATURE

To prepare for the role, Eddie studied how wildlife experts and zoologists track down animals in nature. Spending time with them really impacted the way he portrayed Newt in the movie. "Trackers have to be incredibly silent when they're following an animal," he points out. "One way is to have their feet splayed out so they can place each leg exactly where they want it, in a kind of open stance. That was something I used."

INSPIRED BY REAL ANIMALS

When the film's concept artists were tasked with coming up with the physical details of the Niffler and the other creatures, they looked to nature for inspiration. As producer David Heyman explains, "We realized that, in looking at nature photographs and documentaries, real animals and plants are oftentimes more incredible than what we see in fantasies. So our beasts are fantastic, but they're rooted in the natural world, in terms of their physical attributes and their design."

David Heyman, who also produced the Harry Potter films, says that all of the films' fantastic beasts have one thing in common: "They are all very sympathetic and engaging. Some are witty, some are mischievous, and others are scary—but they all have a kind of humanity as well."

Animated Ideas

The movie's animation director, Pablo Grillo, was involved in the creation of the creatures from the early stages of the project. Pablo has extensive creature design experience and has worked as an animation supervisor on other popular fantasy films, such as the previous Harry Potter movies, *The Golden Compass*, and *Paddington*.

"We wanted Pablo to be involved from the beginning so we could do animation studies for the creature movements that help define them," says David. "It's not just about sculpting them as puppets or as digital creatures. We are blending the processes—which include the sound and the movements—to come up with a creature that you feel might actually exist. It might look extraordinary and do amazing things—but there's a real language and authenticity that goes back to the world that J.K. Rowling has created."

A Beautiful Friendship

Newt Scamander and the Niffler have a very interesting relationship in the movie. Actor Eddie Redmayne used his imagination to conjure up what life would be like carrying the Niffler in his case. He adds, "He's actually one of my favorite beasts, but he does tend to wreak havoc. Things tend to go horribly wrong, and he is this funny catalyst that sets in motion an insane amount of events. He causes a lot of chaos, but I kind of love to hate him."

Playing the part of Newt and trying to see all these fantastic beasts in his mind's eye reminded Eddie of what it was like to play all sorts of pretend games as a young boy. He says, "Your imagination has the most wondrous, frenzied time. I was very lucky to work with these amazing puppeteers and our animation director, Pablo Grillo. Not only is Pablo involved in designing the animals, he is also a wonderful character. He characterizes them physically, and that helps me with the acting a great lot."

✴ ENTERING ✴
NEWT'S MAGICAL CASE

The Niffler and the other magical creatures are all hidden in Newt's enchanted case. As the events of the film demonstrate, if a person were to open Newt's case in its normal setting, the fantastic beasts could escape and create chaos around the city. That's why Newt relies on a unique mechanism to make the case appear normal to No-Majs, such as New York City customs officials. Newt uses the "Muggle Worthy" lock at the Port Authority of New York, so that the case reveals only clothing, binoculars, a map, and other traveler's necessities to the customs official.

To create the magic of the case, production designer Stuart Craig and visual effects supervisor Christian Manz worked very closely to bring J.K. Rowling's vision to life. "You step into a truly magical world," notes Christian. "We're experiencing this with the Jacob Kowalski character, who has stepped through this case and is going through the fantastical, expansive world."

Stuart Craig and Christian Manz worked on many concepts until they came up with the final version of this small world. "It's a mixture of real environments for our heroes to stand in and a magical extension that we're going to create digitally for our magical creatures," says Christian.

JACOB KOWALSKI

Jacob Kowalski is one of the first major characters created by J.K. Rowling who is not a wizard. He is a factory worker who has returned from World War I and dreams of becoming a baker. After the Niffler escapes and he accidentally swaps cases with Newt, Jacob gets mixed up in the hidden magical community in New York. "I really identified with the character because I grew up in New York as well, and I have always been fascinated with the 1920s," says actor Dan Fogler, who plays Jacob. "Being part of this movie has been the greatest job I've ever had in my life."

A NO-MAJ
WITH MAD SKILLS

Audiences will have a great time experiencing the awe-inspiring world of the film through Jacob's eyes, because he's just a regular person. "He's literally the last guy that's back from the war," says Dan. "They told him to keep on digging, and he kept on going, and one day, he looked up and said, 'Where is everybody?' That's when he returned home."

Dan says his character may not have magical powers, but he's got a charming personality. "Jacob loves making people laugh, and he enjoys cooking and baking. He can make a pastry that will knock your socks off. That's kind of magic, right?"

TINA GOLDSTEIN

Porpentina "Tina" Goldstein is another one of the film's fascinating characters who is part of Newt Scamander's circle of new friends. She was formerly an Auror at MACUSA (Magical Congress of the United States of America) but was demoted. She and her sister, Queenie, work at the Wand Permit Office.

GOING BACK IN TIME

Tina is portrayed by actress Katherine Waterston, who has a special affinity for the world of 1920s New York City. "We shoot on this amazing set that has all these fantastic period details and art deco grounds," she says. "We have all this beautiful signage that used to be all over New York back in those days, but so little is left of it today. It's a wonderful experience to go through this time warp and see the world that my grandmother was a part of."

Like many of the other actors working on the movie, Katherine was thrilled to be a part of J.K. Rowling's fantastic universe. "We have to make it seem as if every day is normal and ignore our sense of wonder as we see everything around us," she explains. "It is a little bit hard to shut that down, because it's so entertaining to watch all the other actors, all the other physical work being done, and seeing things flying over their heads and crawling up their arms. It's really just like being a kid and having so much fun."

QUEENIE GOLDSTEIN

Queenie is Tina Goldstein's younger sister. The two women have a very close relationship, as they were orphaned when they were young. A fun-loving and gifted witch, Queenie is a Legilimens, someone who has the ability to read minds, and she is also skilled at using her magical abilities to cook.

Beauty and the Beasts

Queenie's life changes forever after her encounter with Newt and his fantastic creatures. "They're just delightful to play with," says actress Alison Sudol, who plays Queenie. "They may be sort of terrifying at first glance, because you don't know whether they'll bite or they're friendly or what they're made of. But they all have these adorable qualities, and you kind of want to give them a cuddle. That's what Newt brings to these misunderstood creatures—this humanity that lets us see how lovely they are."

A POWERFUL CONNECTION

A huge fan of J.K. Rowling's books, Alison says she felt honored to explore the brand-new territory of the movie: "I think we're all very aware of the legacy of Harry Potter, but what's nice is that this is a new story, something that we're all creating together. It has a strong connection to what's happened before, but it's also its own thing. Moreover, there is so much meaning and heart in Jo's writing—this lack of cynicism—that I really cherish."

THE MAGICAL CONGRESS OF THE UNITED STATES OF AMERICA (MACUSA)

MACUSA, or the Magical Congress of the United States of America, is the US version of Britain's Ministry of Magic. The main offices of this otherworldly group are hidden inside the Woolworth Building in Manhattan.

Standing at 792 feet (241.4 meters), the sixty-story Woolworth Building was the tallest building in the world when it officially opened in 1913. "The outside of the building has neo-Gothic–style decorations," says production designer Stuart Craig. "This whole era was such a time of fantastic contrast. It was when modernism really got underway."

THE MACUSA SEAL

The official MACUSA seal features a stylized phoenix—a symbol of renewal and immortality—and an American flag with forty-eight stars, as at the time of the movie Alaska and Hawaii were not yet states.

Lessons from History

Four golden phoenix statues are located in the lobby of the **MACUSA** building. Also on display is a statue of four adults and a child—a memorial to the victims of the Salem Witch Trials. The statue serves as a reminder of the persecution that No-Majs inflicted upon the American witches and wizards in the past. Stuart explains, "It is important that the magical world is grounded in the context of the Muggle world, born out of things familiar and real."

Details, Details!

The artists and craftsmen who helped design and build the intricate architectural features of the **MACUSA** building were quite aware of all the elements that make a set come alive on camera. The small props that reveal the everyday details of the wizarding world were high on the list. The fact that the desks have light sources that don't sit on them but levitate slightly is one of those intricate details. "A favorite of mine is the wand polisher," Stuart adds. "It's operated by a house-elf who puts the wand into big ostrich-feather buffers and also sinks his arm in. When he withdraws it, his arm's shiny!"

PERCIVAL GRAVES

★ ★ ★ ★ ★ ★ ★ ★ ★ ★

Acclaimed Irish actor Colin Farrell portrays Percival Graves in the movie. His character is a powerful Auror and the Director of Magical Security for MACUSA. He says he was thrilled to be part of J.K. Rowling's fantastic world and wished he had been asked to play a part before. "To be part of this world is a really cool thing. J.K. Rowling creates beautiful worlds, and I had a lot of fun doing it."

He also enjoyed the experience of working with director David Yates and the rest of the actors. "David is an extraordinary man and filmmaker who feels like the protector of the kingdom. He is so well versed in the mythology of that world and has a deep affinity for the characters and the lore. He was great to be around."

PRACTICING HIS CRAFT

To brush up on his wand-waving skills, Colin was given an antique orchestra conductor's baton to practice with when he wasn't filming. "I would walk around my hotel room in my bathrobe with that [baton] in my hand," he admits. Colin adds that he would make elaborate wand moves and pretend he was using magic to turn on his TV.

A Mysterious Relationship

Percival has a relationship with Credence Barebone (played by Ezra Miller), who is the adopted son of Mary Lou Barebone, the head of the New Salem Philanthropic Society. While seemingly supportive, Graves's motivations for befriending Credence are unclear. Colin explains, "Credence is a young man who, like so many young men, seems lost in his life. It seems like the world is a mystery to him, so he is a mystery to himself as well. So Graves provides a little bit of guidance, a little bit of support and tenderness, and a little bit of manipulation."

Clothes Make the Man

In the movie, Graves wears a very long coat with exaggerated shoulders. Created by award-winning designer Colleen Atwood, the character's costumes were mostly dark, with a black-and-white edge to them so that he stands out among the other colorful costumes and sets. The stark simplicity of his coat also reflects his straightforward attitude and structured world.

MAKE IT YOUR OWN

Before you start building and decorating your model, read through the included instruction sheet. Then, choose a theme and make a plan. The choice is yours! Here is a sample project to get those creative juices flowing.

Attracted to all sorts of shiny things, the Niffler has been known to leave destruction in its wake. To avoid the perils of having a Niffler loose in your home, try out this project instead. You can now create your very own adorable, yet stationary, Niffler.

What You Need
- Paintbrush
- Black, peach/flesh tone, gold, orange-brown, gray, and pink paint

What You Might Want
- Water-based gouache paint
- Metallic gold pen

Tips
- Gouache paint is a type of opaque watercolor. It blends nicely and coats the wood well. If you don't have gouache, acrylic paint will work as well.

- It is a lot easier to paint the Niffler before you build it. You might also want to paint the coins (piece 42) separately and then attach when dry.

1. Start by painting the entire model black. Make sure you get all the nooks and crannies. Let it dry completely.

2. Paint the coins gold and set aside. You can also use a metallic pen for this part.

3. Once the black paint is completely dry, paint flesh-colored circles around the eyes.

4. Paint the entire snout flesh-colored as well. Blend the paint so the eye circles are connected to the snout.

5. Paint the very tip of the snout pink.

6. Dab a little orange-brown paint onto the snout and blend the paint to create a gradient. It should go from orange-brown to flesh-colored, as seen in the photo.

7. Paint the inside edge of the eyes orange-brown.

8. Paint the claws on the Niffler's hands and feet brown, but paint the rest of the hands and feet flesh-colored.

9. Dab some orange-brown paint onto each hand and foot. Blend the paint so there is a gradient from dark to light, just as you did on the snout.

10. Add small brushstrokes in a medium-gray color all over the Niffler's body for the fur.

11. To finish, use a slightly lighter gray to paint the tips of all the medium-gray brushstrokes.

IncrediBuilds™
A Division of Insight Editions LP
PO Box 3088
San Rafael, CA 94912
www.insighteditions.com

Find us on Facebook: www.facebook.com/InsightEditions
Follow us on Twitter: @insighteditions

Published by Insight Editions, San Rafael, California, in 2016.
No part of this book may be reproduced in any form without
written permission from the publisher.

Library of Congress Cataloging-in-Publication Data available.

ISBN: 978-1-68298-061-3

Publisher: Raoul Goff
Art Director: Chrissy Kwasnik
Designer: Leah Bloise
Executive Editor: Vanessa Lopez
Project Editor: Greg Solano
Associate Editor: Katie DeSandro
Production Editor: Elaine Ou
Production Manager: Thomas Chung
Production Coordinators: Sam Taylor and Leeana Diaz
Model Design: Liang Tujian, Team Green

INSIGHT EDITIONS would like to thank David Heyman, Victoria Selover,
Melanie Swartz, Elaine Piechowski, Margo Guffin, Kevin Morris,
Jill Benscoter, Niki Judd, Gina Cavalier, Kate Cellan-Jones, and Nick Gligor.

Insight Editions, in association with Roots of Peace, will plant two trees
for each tree used in the manufacturing of this book. Roots of Peace is
an internationally renowned humanitarian organization dedicated to
eradicating land mines worldwide and converting war-torn lands into
productive farms and wildlife habitats. Roots of Peace will plant two
million fruit and nut trees in Afghanistan and provide farmers there with
the skills and support necessary for sustainable land use.

Manufactured in Shaoguan, China, by Insight Editions

10 9 8 7 6 5 4 3 2